True Wisdom

True Wisdom

Ten Precious Guidelines from Bowang Sammaeron

for a Happy Life

By Ven. Pomnyun Sunim

JUNGTO

True Wisdom

by Ven. Pomnyun Sunim

Copyright © 2013 by Ven. Pomnyun Sunim
All rights reserved.
Except in the case of brief quotations,
no part of the this book may be reproduced in any form
without written permission from the publisher.

JUNGTO Publishing
1585-16, Seocho-3dong, Seocho-gu, Seoul, South Korea / +82-2-587-8991
4361 Aitcheson Rd. Beltsville, MD 20705 USA /+1-240-786-7528

Website : www.jungto.org
email : book@jungto.org

Printed in South Korea
First Edition : Summer, 2013

Photo by Moonsun Lee, Youngsook Park

ISBN 978-89-85961-80-6 03810

CONTENTS

In recent times, earning a living and satisfying our basic needs, such as food, clothing and shelter, have become a struggle. Nothing – job, friends, or family – seems to go our way. Each day we encounter all kinds of depressing news.

However, when we look at things from a different perspective, we can be thankful that we are alive today, can put food on our tables and have clothes to wear. Also, our gait becomes lighter on our way home from work because we have a loving family and good neighbors. This very moment, while we are living our day to its fullest, is the happiest time of our lives. If we keep such a positive outlook on life, we can be happy every day, even if we get sick and encounter hardships.

Ven. Pomnyun Sunim shows us how we can lead joyful lives by incorporating the teachings in Bowang Sammaeron, "Ten Actions That Help Practice," into our everyday lives. Ven. Pomnyun Sunim explains each of the ten guidelines using examples that readers can easily relate to. These timeless guidelines teach us that with a positive outlook, we can be free and happy with things just the way they are without having to change the world. I hope this book will help you get many steps closer to a new life filled with happiness.

Summer, 2013
Jungto Publishing Co.

Explanatory notes :

Bowang Sammaeron , "Ten Actions That Help Practice," is the 17th of 22 passages in "Bowang Sammae Chanting of Buddha's Teachings," written by Ven. Mohyup Sunim of China. This book consists of Ven. Pomnyun Sunim's explanation of Bowang Sammaeron in the form of the ten guidelines that can be applied to make our lives happy.

Consider illness as your medicine

Do not wish for perfect health.

Perfect health makes it easy for you to be greedy.

Thus, the Buddha said,

"Consider illness as your medicine."

We all want to be healthy but none of us can avoid having illnesses. This is the fundamental suffering of mankind. In Buddhism, fundamental human suffering is represented by four things: birth, aging, sickness and death. If we are born, we will ultimately die. Despite the fact that everyone who is born must die, people wish to live forever. Inevitably, they suffer as they yearn for the impossible.

Death is considered suffering only because we view it as such. But if we see it from a different perspective, it is simply a phenomenon. Death is one of the phenomena of nature just as the formation of the waves is a feature of the ocean, and leaves sprouting in Spring and leaves falling in Autumn are characteristics of the seasons. Would you regard the dancing of the waves to be suffering? Would you consider the falling of the leaves a form of torment? No, they are natural phenomena, and we cannot say that they are "good," "bad," "joyful," or "painful."

We humans are imprisoned by our own thoughts, so we do not acknowledge birth, aging, sickness and death as natural occurrences, and we suffer as a result. Even at this very instant, countless natural phenomena are occurring in the world. We celebrate them as principles of life: we celebrate the budding of leaves in the Spring, the blooming of flowers in the Summer, and the coloring of leaves in the Autumn.

Nevertheless, we are unwilling to acknowledge the natural course of action when it comes to our own bodies. If we view the world in a detached manner, birth, aging, sickness and death are simply natural phenomena. However, we suffer because we are so attached to our bodies and don't accept these stages as the logical course of our lives. Therefore, if we know the teachings of the Dharma, that is, if we can see things as they truly are, we should not wish to avoid illness since becoming ill is just a natural phenomenon.

The human body is much like a machine. Any machine can sometimes have problems, and no machine can be trouble free forever. We may hope that it won't break down, but that doesn't mean it will not happen. When a machine malfunctions, there is inevitably a cause. Thus, instead of becoming irritable, we just need to fix the broken machine. After a certain period of time, however, the machine won't be reparable. When the cost of repair outweighs the value of the machine, it is better to dispose of it. Since you have gotten the full use out of it, it is not a loss to discard it.

When our car has frequent breakdowns, we are able to find out about its condition and exercise more caution when operating it. If a car often has problems, we are less likely to speed. On the contrary, if the car is trouble-free, we may drive it more recklessly. If we speed, the probability of dying in an accident increases. It is the same with our bodies. In extreme cases, people who have never experienced an illness in their lives may die once they get sick and are hospitalized the first time. It is rare for a person who has never been sick to enjoy longevity. There is a Korean saying, "People with minor illnesses end up living longer," because they are more

inclined to take care of their bodies in a timely fashion. On the other hand, individuals who rarely get sick tend to become overly confident about their bodies, so they are more likely to, one day, find themselves diagnosed with a serious disease.

Generally speaking, when you have perfect health, it is easy to become greedy. What is greed? Is it wanting to eat when hungry and wanting to sleep when tired? No, these are basic desires rather than covetousness. But when desires are too strong, they turn into greed. There are five types of desires people have: the desire for food, sex, money, sleep and prestige. If we are healthy, these cravings become stronger, and we become greedy, and we are more likely to enjoy a lifestyle that is conducive to developing illnesses. That is why people without an illness may easily become greedy.

If we become ill, we need to search for the cause. If we look carefully, we can definitely find one. Because we often don't know the cause, we tend to think a great misfortune has befallen us. When we become ill, it is important to take the opportunity to examine and reflect on the way we have been living our lives. Praying provides us with a time of reflection. It is not about prostrating a few times at the temple. True prayer is about making an effort to realize the "emptiness" of everything and rid ourselves of greed. Only when this happens can our illness serve us as medicine, giving us an impetus to critically reflect on our lives for repentance.

This can only be possible if we don't fear illness. A body is born, ages, becomes ill and dies. During this natural course, it is inevitable that we will become sick at some point. In Vimalakirti Sutra[1], Yuma[2] used his illness as a means of teaching the Dharma. He did not pray to be cured. He simply helped people realize the Truth that their bodies will eventually succumb to disease. He tells us to become aware that illness is caused by greed and that we can be cured by letting go of it. Thus, based on the fundamental teachings of the Buddha, we should be unhindered by illness, regardless of whether or not we become ill.

Moreover, when we get sick, we shouldn't react in an overly sensitive manner, but rather, take it lightly, thinking, "The body should be well-maintained, but it can sometimes have problems." If we become sick,

1. Vimalakirti Sutra : A popular and influential Mahayana Buddhist scripture that teaches the concept of non-duality. It features a teaching addressed to high-ranking Buddhist disciples through the mouth of layman bodhisattva Vimalakirti.

2. Yuma : Korean name for layman bodhisattva Vimalakirti who teaches the concept of non-duality in Vimalakirti Sutra.

we should treat the sickness without drama and move on with our lives. Also, there is always a cause for an illness, so we need to find out what it is and treat it. However, if you go to the hospital and receive a bad diagnosis, you should not dwell on the cause of the illness too much.

In today's society, 80 percent of our illnesses are caused by stress, overeating, and other indulgences. Thus, we should be less self-indulgent and greedy and be more carefree and generous. The harder we seek the things we want and cling to our possessions, the more our bodies and minds will suffer and become sick. This is especially true with our relationships concerning immediate family members. The more we demand that our spouses, children, or parents follow our wishes, the more stressful our lives become, making us more likely to become ill. Therefore, when we can deeply respect the wishes of our family members and everyone else by trying to see things from their points of view and acknowledge their opinions, we can become happy and healthy.

Accept your worries and hardships as part of life

Do not wish for a life free from hardships.

Such a life only leads to arrogance and self-pampering.

Thus, the Buddha said,

"Accept your worries and hardships as part of life."

Living in this world, we often experience difficulties. At the beginning of each year, Koreans visit famous Buddhist temples to pray for a safe year that is free from adversity. Wishing to escape misfortune, they visit great Buddhist temples deep in the mountains all over Korea to pray. However, Ten Actions That Help Practice, known as "Bowang Sammaeron" in Korean, tells us not to seek a life without hardships.

Having a body means that we will inevitably become ill someday, despite our wish to remain healthy. Likewise, in the world in which we live, things rarely go our way. If everyone's wishes were granted, chaos would reign. People desire different things that are in conflict with each other. Let's say a person wants to become a monk with the goal of attaining enlightenment. However, his parents and girlfriend may be wishing for something different for his future. What would happen if the three conflicting wishes of these individuals were all granted at the same time?

People wish for clear skies when they plan an outdoor activity. However, if we lived in a world in which everyone's wishes were granted, we would have sunny weather continually because there's bound to be someone planning an outing on any given day. Then, farming would be impossible due to a water shortage. So, you can see that having all your dreams come true is not particularly desirable. Wanting everything to go your way is no different from wishing the world

to collapse. In adherence to the nature of the world we live in, sometimes our desires will be granted and sometimes not; this is the Truth. However, since we tend to think all our wishes should come true, when they don't, we are unhappy and have a hard time accepting reality.

Two views exist with respect to the many difficulties we experience in our lives. One is the view of causality (cause and effect), which contends that the hardships we encounter result from the causes we create unbeknownst to us, so we should accept hardships without complaint. Everything that happens in the world follows the principle of causality, so there is always a cause for every outcome. Unenlightened people don't realize that they themselves have created the cause of the effect. Consequently, they regard the result as a misfortune or a difficulty. However, if we know the cause of a situation, we can realize that it is just a natural outcome. When we realize the law of causality, we can accept reality more easily and free ourselves from suffering.

The other view asserts that everything simply follows its natural course. More specifically, it is normal that things do not go our way, so there is no reason to be distressed when they don't. Thus, whether the skies are clear or cloudy, these facts in themselves cannot be reasons for suffering. The rain does not fall nor does the sun shine with the intention of making us suffer. They are simply weather conditions that change from day to day; it is only when we insist on either rain or sunshine that things become problematic. We feel unhappy when things don't go our way. However, we wouldn't feel that way if we didn't have any expectations. Then, events not turning out the way we want would simply be a little inconvenient. The important point here is that, in reality, our wishes will not always be granted, so we should not feel distressed when they are not. In sum, since it is normal that things don't go our way, believing otherwise will make us suffer.

However, on rare occasions, it can seem as though things are turning out just the way we want. People can feel that way when they suddenly become rich or famous, and as a result, they may become reckless and conceited. We can see this in others as well as in ourselves. When everything goes our way, we grow arrogant and boastful. Then, invariably, we feel superior and oppress others. This is why the Buddha insisted that all practitioners subsist on alms. How can people who rely on the generosity of others for sustenance be arrogant? They must lower their heads at people's doors every day to obtain food.

They have to humbly accept their circumstances, whether or not they are given food and whether the portion is small or large. Also, they must appreciate any kind of food offered to them. Requesting alms and begging for food are two different things. The request for alms by practitioners is a way of spiritual practice, while begging is a means of satisfying one's desires. The former act requires the extinguishment of greed, while the latter is fueled by avarice. Also, the person who asks for alms humbly awaits the decision of the one having the food on whether any will be donated. On the other hand, the person who begs is coercing the giver to donate food, whether by physical force or by relentless solicitation. Thus, one has to be humble to subsist on alms given by others, which is why the Buddha asked practitioners to do so.

The Buddha said, "Be humble, not servile.

Be proud, not arrogant." People often find it difficult to differentiate between humility and servility. The distinguishing factor is greed. We become servile when we are driven by our greed but can be humble when we are not. Since good practitioners are free from greed, they are proudly humble and humbly proud at the same time. Therefore, they can be bold as well as humble in front of anyone. However, ordinary people tend to be subservient to those they consider superior while being boastful to those they regard as inferior. For example, people who are attached to money are servile to those who have more money than they do, while they look down on people with less. Also, individuals who covet power abase themselves before those in higher positions while they behave arrogantly in front of those in lower positions. Similarly, people who value physical appearance are self-conscious in front of those who are more attractive, but are pretentious in front of those less attractive. Finally, those who prize knowledge are diffident before those more knowledgeable than they and are scornful of those with less intelligence. We behave this way because, unfortunately, that is how our minds work. If we let go of the notion of "slef" or the ego, there will be no reason for us to be either servile or arrogant toward others.

The Buddha had practitioners obtain alms from the poor in order to teach them to be humble toward the poor and forbade them from asking for alms at palaces in order to teach them not to be subservient even to kings. Most of us will lower our heads before kings and hold our heads up in front of the poor. However, the Buddha taught us to do the contrary. He told practitioners to place the people with the highest social status under their feet and those with the lowest social status on top of their heads, thereby teaching them to view everyone in the world as equals. He did not mean that practitioners should debase kings and exalt the poor. Rather, the Buddha taught them to "be humble, not arrogant; be proud, not servile" in the sense that they should treat everyone equally.

Moreover, the Buddha taught us to carefully observe our reactions to the external conditions that bring us hardships and realize that they are illusions. There is no such thing as hardship per se; adversity is created because of our desire for everything to turn out the way we want. Even when what we regard as hardship arises, if we understand that it does not inherently exist, that it is "empty," we won't be emotionally affected by it. Realizing that difficulties do not actually exist, but have been created in our heads, allows us to not be hindered by them.

Attain Nirvana amidst the hindrances

Do not wish to be free of hindrances in your practice.

Without hindrances,

it will be hard to advance in your practice.

Thus, the Buddha said,

"Attain Nirvana amidst the hindrances."

Wouldn't it be wonderful if we could concentrate on chanting when we chant, if the subject of meditation would get more vivid when practicing Zen meditation, and we could focus only on our breathing when meditating? However, in reality, this is far from what we experience when we practice.

When we practice, we have a hard time staying focused because we are distracted by all kinds of emotional afflictions and delusions. Generally, hindrances along the spiritual path can be divided into two categories: internal and external. When we encounter external obstacles such as the passing of parents or the bankruptcy of a family business, it becomes difficult to continue with our practice despite our resolve to do so. However, an external hindrance should be regarded simply as an incident rather than an obstacle. Otherwise, an external incident can make us doubt the validity of our practice, undermining our resolve to practice. If we let an external obstacle make us skeptical about our practice and dwell on the negative feelings, the external obstacle suddenly becomes an internal one. Therefore, I will not talk about external hindrances here since they are actually not obstacles in the true sense of the word. When we don't have self-doubts about our practice, external hindrances in fact, help our practice by making us work harder.

The first internal hindrance we face in our practice is our emotional afflictions. When we sit down to meditate, thoughts about our past arise in an endless stream. Even though the past is just a record of events which we cannot change, we still dwell on the past much of the time. This is the problem. When we have a grudge against the world and people, we continue to harbor animosity toward them for a long time. Ironically, holding onto pleasant memories about the past can also cause emotional afflictions to arise. If we become attached to thoughts such as, "I used to have a high social position, I used to be rich, I used to be beautiful…" we become dissatisfied with our present state. Dwelling on happy memories of the past, we neglect the things we must do now, which makes us unhappy with our present lives. Likewise, ruminating about unpleasant memories of the past also makes our present lives unhappy.

The second hindrance is delusion. Delusions are thoughts about what might happen in the future. Imagining that certain things will happen, even though it is unlikely, makes us anxious. In short, we are anxious and unhappy in the present because we worry about what might happen in the future.

The third hindrance is skepticism. We question ourselves, "What is the use of practice? What is the use of prostrating?" Furthermore, we doubt our own faith in spiritual practice with nagging thoughts such as "Why do I have to practice?", "Why do I have to repent?" These kinds of doubts keep forming in our minds. If we keep thinking about not wanting to practice, we eventually succeed in coming up with a valid reason not to. Thus, we end up discontinuing our practice and feeling justified in doing so. We delude ourselves into thinking that being unable to practice is beyond our control since the reasons to discontinue are so compelling. Skepticism and doubts that arise while we practice are powerful hindrances. Even though emotional afflictions hinder our practice by preventing us from staying focused, they are not so detrimental as to make us completely stop practicing. However, skepticism and doubt can do just that by making us seriously question, "Is practice really necessary? Isn't it OK to not practice?" These thoughts usually occur when there are changes in our external situation such as moving to another house or going on a long trip.

The fourth hindrance is aversion. When we are consumed by our dislike of something, we can neither hear what others say nor see anything clearly. When we are taken over by an intense abhorrence of something, we lose objectivity, and we can no longer understand

others. Thus, aversion is the most detrimental among all the attachments that plague us. It is also the most powerful of all hindrances.

Finally, the fifth and last hindrance is despair. Having no will to do anything and being in a daze are major obstacles in spiritual practice. The things we consider as hindrances are not real hindrances, but in our minds we perceive them as such. Thus, things occurring in the external world are, in reality, simply incidents. We need to be aware of the feelings arising in our minds and realize how strongly our karma influences what we like and dislike. Then, we wouldn't be so attached to our feelings, which are mere reflections of our deeply ingrained karma.

It would be great if everything we did turned out the way we wanted so that we are able to meditate serenely observe our breathing once we sit down to meditate and stay focused on the mantra once we begin to chant. Unfortunately, when things come too easily, we become arrogant. We should not take the easy road in everything we do. A reasonable number of hindrances gives us an opportunity to persevere, which makes us stronger and centered. Thus, experiencing hindrances in life is not a bad thing. If we cannot overcome the hindrance, we will fall into despair, but if we are able to, we can make significant progress in our practice. It is much like running an obstacle course. For example, If you successfully clear the obstacles, you win. However, if you cannot jump over the obstacles and fall down, you lose. Once you have vowed to practice, you need to overcome whatever hindrances you encounter along the path.

If we understand that all hindrances are insubstantial and empty by nature, we will no longer experience hindrances. Something becomes a hindrance only when we are hindered by it. To reiterate, when we are not affected by an obstacle, it is no longer a hindrance. Instead, it is simply an incident. As stated in the Heart Sutra[3], "If hindrance disappears from the mind, external hindrance will also vanish, and without hindrance, there is nothing to be afraid of."

No matter how much we wish to be free of hindrances, they will always be part of our lives. If the mind is caught up in feelings of dislike about something, this state of mind becomes a hindrance. If the mind is not hindered, that "something" will simply be an incident. When we are able to overcome our negative feelings about the incident, we will become more competent and have more equanimity in our

---

3. Heart Sutra : The shortest and most famous sutra in Mahayana Buddhism. Regarded as the summation of the wisdom of the Buddha, the sutra explains the concept of non-attachment and emptiness.

lives. In fact, when we look back, many hardships we experienced in the past have helped us mature and make progress in our practice. In the end, they turned out to be blessings in disguise. Obstacles act as catalysts in our path toward enlightenment. Thus, we should attain Nirvana through hindrances. Finally, we need to be free amidst hindrances because without them we cannot obtain true freedom.

Treat temptation as a friend
who helps you in your practice

Do not hope to be free from temptation in your practice.

Without temptations, your resolve cannot become strong.

Thus, the Buddha said,

"Treat temptation as a friend who helps you in your practice."

Many people experience temptation in their practice. This means various internal obstacles that hinder their practice occur. We all wish to be free from temptations, but we are often plagued by them. In the past, people believed temptation to be an external obstacle. However, it is an internal obstacle we have created in our minds. Whatever happens outside our minds is simply an incident. However, if we let our minds be adversely affected by it, it can become a real obstacle in our practice.

Why do our minds resist rather than go forward when we are trying to do something? It is because of our habits, also known as karmic consciousness. When we try to change the habits we have had for a long time, there is a lot of resistance. The principle of karmic flow is the same as that of the Law of Inertia, Newton's First Law of Motion. An object in motion has a tendency to continue moving in the same direction at the same speed, while an object at rest has a tendency to remain at rest. Thus, in order to stop an object in motion, we must apply force to it. Likewise, we need to apply a strong force to make a stationary object move. Our habits behave the same way. Because our behavior patterns tend to persist as they have until now, they will resist strongly when we try to change them. Most of us cannot overcome this resistance. For instance, even when we are determined to change our

habits, something always seems to get in the way which undermines our resolve. This is why there is an old Korean saying, "A resolution lasts no longer than three days."

However, temptation can disappear without a trace when we have "Great Determination," being firm enough in our resolve to be ready to die for it. On the other hand, if there is even a tiny crack in our resolve, temptation will find its way in and take over. Temptations will tantalize and persuade us until we are convinced that we don't need to practice.

Also, hesitation and doubt can distract our minds when we try to make a decision. Even the Buddha was tempted by "Ma-Wang (the King of Temptation)" right up to the moment of his enlightenment under the Bodhi tree. He was offered the opportunity to be the King of Temptation and have almighty power. This would be what most ordinary people would dream of. However, the Buddha responded, "King of Temptation, there is nothing that I wish for." Since there was nothing he wanted, temptation could not affect him.

Let's think about this carefully. Is it better to have all our wishes granted or not to have any wishes in the first place? As odd as it may sound, not wanting anything is actually much better. For example, if we do not wish for the weather to be a certain way, it won't matter to us if the day is wet, cloudy, hot or cold. However if we wish for a specific weather, we will be either happy or disappointed depending on the meteorological condition of the day. Thus, if we reflect on this, we will see that the Buddha's teachings give us great insight and wisdom.

In the Dharma, there is no discrimination of

high or low. This is because all beings are equal, and they are neither inherently more valuable nor less valuable than others. All things by nature are "empty," meaning devoid of an intrinsically fixed worth. That is, we assign the value of something according to how useful it is to our needs at the time. However, we mistakenly believe that things have inherent "high" or "low" values based on our self-created value system. Thus, we get attached to the idea that certain things are more or less valuable than others. It is important to never lose sight of the Truth of all things, that they are impermanent and empty in essence. Only then will we be able to pick ourselves up and stay on the right path regardless of how many times we may stumble and fall. Otherwise, we won't even know when we are doing something wrong, which leaves us unable to ask questions when we need to. Once we have realized the Truth, we will at least know when we have done something wrong and be aware of our ignorance when we don't know something. As a result, we will experience progress in our practice as time goes by. We need to have a clear understanding of the Truth.

Even after understanding the Truth, we unconsciously revert to our old habits because they are so hard to change. Since our habits seem to take over whenever we are not vigilant, it is very difficult to act in accordance with the Truth. This is the point where we should begin our spiritual practice. Practice is getting up again and again each time we fall down. Staying down after we have fallen is not practice. Therefore, practice is a continuous process. If there are no obstacles along the path, it will be hard to advance in our practice. Just as we become arrogant when our wishes are easily fulfilled, if our practice is smooth sailing, we can become conceited, thinking that we've reached a certain level of enlightenment when we actually haven't.

Rather than wishing for no temptation, we should be able to overcome the snares we encounter along the path. It is important to be aware when temptation arises within us and recognize it as such. We have to observe how it crops up, contemplating, "Ah, this is my old habit at work again. This is how temptation arises. Let's see how deep the root of my old habits is." That way, we won't surrender so easily to temptations. As we advance in our practice and gain the ability to perceive the Truth, we can see clearly how often we deviate from the right path. We can vigilantly observe ourselves at all times, while interacting with our spouses, eating, sleeping and prostrating. Every hour of our day can be the object of our practice.

It's good when we are doing well with our practice. However, even when it seems like we are failing and making mistakes, it still serves us well because it gives us the opportunity to repent and learn not to make the same mistake again. This is why we should simply get up when we have fallen. If we are clearly aware of what makes us stumble, we may falter once or twice, but there is a good chance we won't fall down the third time. Just as it is normal for the world to be chaotic, it is only natural that there are obstacles along the path. Thus, temptation is an inherent part of practice. Without temptation, our resolve cannot be firm. If we fall down ten thousand times but are still willing to stand back up again, our resolve is substantial. If the Buddha didn't have such a firm resolve, he might have been seduced by Ma-Wang's offer of almighty power over the entire world.

If we can clearly see with the eyes of wisdom that temptation is only an illusion, it cannot make us suffer. We should not wish temptation away. If we are able to reflect, "Ah, I am tempted by this, so this is what I need to overcome in my practice." experiencing temptation will give us the opportunity for further self-discovery. Then, thanks to temptation, we may find what we need to focus on in our practice. Therefore, instead of wishing to be free of temptation, I hope you will make good use of it as a means for furthering your practice.

Persevere through long periods of time to accomplish your goals

Do not wish for things to work out easily.

When things work out easily, one becomes rash.

Thus, the Buddha said,

"Persevere through many lifetimes to accomplish your goals."

Whenever we set out to do something, we all wish to accomplish it easily. However, more often than not, things don't go our way. When things are not going well, we get frustrated and blame ourselves. On the other hand, when things do go our way, we tend to overestimate our abilities, taking on tasks we cannot possibly handle.

If we climb a mountain that is not challenging, it may be easy to ascend but probably not that exciting, whereas if we go hiking up a rugged mountain, it will be challenging but also fun. In addition, rather than climbing the same peak every time, trying a mountain you have never climbed before will be even more exhilarating. When we get lost on a mountain, it is stressful at the time. However, looking back on the experience, we realize that we wouldn't have become so familiar with the terrain if we hadn't gotten lost. Likewise, when we have a setback while working, we can explore different ways of approaching the task, gaining more experience and knowledge and consequently becoming experts in that field.

However, if we do not make an effort to figure out the reasons for our failure, we end up frustrated and disappointed. Sometimes, we pray to higher beings such as God or the Buddha in the hopes of solving the problem without much effort on our part, but that is not the right way. When things don't work out, we must figure out the reasons for the failure and turn the experience into an opportunity for learning. In addition, we should never carry out a given job carelessly, without preparation, and irresponsibly say, "I will just use this opportunity to further my practice," when we fail. However, despite the meticulous planning, sometimes external circumstances do not cooperate with what we want to accomplish. In the cases in which we have done everything possible to prepare, we won't be disappointed, but rather, we will be able to view the failed task as the object of further study and research.

In fact, experiencing unexpected situations a few times may enable us to become experts in a particular area and may help us develop the ability to respond to changing circumstances in the future. In short, failures can be valuable learning lessons. On the other hand, when things go smoothly, we become overly confident and complacent. Then, we are likely to be negligent in preparing for unexpected situations and could even end up feeling overwhelmed or in despair when faced with obstacles. Just as a person with many minor illnesses has more experience dealing with sickness, a person with ample failures has greater capability to cope with problems.

Jungto Society takes a Buddhist pilgrimage to India every year. When more than a hundred people travel together, unexpected things are bound to happen. Unforeseen situations can occur in spite of meticulous planning and preparations. For instance, we have had to spend an unscheduled night in Bangkok because dense fog prevented the plane from taking off. Also, because India's culture is very different from that of Korea, many things which do not make sense to us

can happen. Therefore, we begin with the assumption that problems will occur and think ahead about what we can do to solve them. For example, when we create the itinerary for the pilgrimage, we try to keep in mind that the train could be delayed seven to eight hours or the bus could break down in the middle of the trip. We prepare a plan that will enable us to respond to those possible situations without major disruptions in our itinerary. Therefore, we construct the itinerary with enough flexibility to accommodate last-minute changes. For instance, if our plane is scheduled to arrive in India in the evening, we spend the next day sightseeing during the day and plan on taking the train in the evening. That way, should the plane be delayed, we can easily skip sightseeing and catch the train to go to the next destination.

The most trying incident we had in India was

when we arrived at the hotel and were told that the rooms we had reserved were not available. It turned out that the hotel had given our rooms to other travelers who had paid double the price. To prepare the pilgrimage participants for such unexpected situations, we inform them at the orientation that, "When we arrive in India, many things will not go according to our plans, and we have to accept the unexpected changes as they occur." Rather than complain about the inconvenience as we would when traveling for leisure with a travel agency, it is important to have a positive attitude during the pilgrimage, even if we end up sleeping in the street for a night or two. That is why we must remain focused on our practice at all times, even on the bus and the train during the pilgrimage. Also, the person in charge of the pilgrimage must always regard the safety and comfort of the participants as a high priority. Thus, this person now arrives at the hotel four to five hours before the participants to check on the reservation and confirm that everything is in order. We were able to put in place these kinds of precautionary measures thanks to the difficulties we experienced in the past.

We should not think that it is good to always have things go our way. If everything progresses effortlessly, we become impulsive and arrogant, feeling superior to others. When we are planning to do something, we should not wish for smooth sailing. We can execute our plans as intended, but the outcome is decided by the combination of numerous factors rather than our intentions alone. This is the principle of cause, condition and effect, more commonly known as "cause and effect." "Cause" is the intention, and "condition" is the given circumstances. Even when the cause is weak, the outcome will be strong if the given condition is good.

Let's take electricity as an example. An electrical spark alone, if it doesn't happen to touch a tree or an object nearby, won't start a fire. Without the proper surrounding conditions, the spark cannot become a flame. Likewise, if there is no spark, there won't be a fire even in a fire hazard environment. However, a spark and flammable objects combined will ignite a big blaze, if no one is there to extinguish it. This is what we call "the principle of cause, condition and effect." Carefully setting up a good plan is the "cause." The cause is like a seed. Having a good seed is helpful, but not all good seeds grow well. If it lands on gravel, it won't sprout. Thus, the result largely depends on the "condition." When a good seed lands on gravel, we have to move it to fertile soil. On the other hand, if the soil is good but the seed is bad, we have to find a viable seed to plant.

Finally, we are the ones doing the work, but we must realize that things don't always turn out the way we intended since the surrounding circumstances also affect the outcome. Again, a task is accomplished not just by our own abilities but in combination with the surrounding conditions, so it is important to have the strength to cope with all kinds of outcomes. Therefore, consider the various difficulties you experience while doing a job as part of your practice, and enjoy the process of overcoming them as they arise.

Preserve your friendship
with pure motives

Do not wish to benefit from your friendships.

Seeking to benefit from your friends

will damage the friendship.

Thus, the Buddha said,

"Preserve your friendship with pure motives."

When we befriend someone, we try to benefit from him or her in some way. A "good friend" is a "friend who benefits me," and this "benefit" is not solely limited to financial gain. We all like friends who are advantageous to us in different ways: provide us with useful information, give us financial help, connect us with the right people for our careers, or entertain us with their fun personalities. However, if a friend whines and complains every day and burdens us by asking us to lend him or her money, we tend to distance ourselves from that friend.

The same is true for married couples. People get married with the intention of reaping benefits from their spouses. When they realize that they have little to gain from the marriage after living together for a while, they think "I would be better off living alone." Concluding that being married isn't better than being single means they were not able to reap as many benefits as they wanted from their marriage. Furthermore, when a person resorts to saying, "I cannot live with my spouse any longer," it means he or she has incurred a loss from the marriage.

A long time ago, I conducted a workshop for married couples in Korea. At the time, I asked the wives, "What do you want most from your husbands, and what do you think your husbands want most from you?" Then I asked the same questions to the husbands, "What do you want most from your wives, and what do you think your wives want most from you?" Surprisingly enough, the answer the wives gave as to what they wanted most from their husbands was self-respect, not money. Apparently, living as married couples, the wives had frequently felt emotionally hurt because their husbands disrespected and degraded them. They said they felt most humiliated when their husbands belittled them in front of their own children by saying things like, "What do you know? You don't know anything."

When I asked the husbands what they thought their wives wanted most from them, "money" was the top answer. They said the only thing that came to their minds when they thought of their wives was money, and they believed their wives were content as long as they brought their salaries home. Since the husbands were under so much pressure to earn money, they suffered from low self-esteem when they didn't earn enough. On the other hand, some of the husbands who earned high salaries tended to cheat on their wives. Since they believed they had fulfilled their duties as husbands by bringing in enough income for their families. As a result, they didn't feel guilty about being unfaithful to their wives, and they felt entitled to do anything they wished. Therefore, in order for husbands and wives in Korea to be equals, wives must dispel the stereotype that husbands have to be the breadwinners in the family. Equality between men and women includes sharing the financial responsibility as well. When a husband loses his job, the wife should seek employment and assume the responsibility of supporting the family. If she resents her husband for losing his job and thinks of him as incompetent, their marriage is not an egalitarian one. If wives argue they are the weaker gender only when it is advantageous for them but demand equal rights when it is disadvantageous, they are bound to get into conflicts with their husbands.

Realistically, we have to accept the fact that people form friendships when they have something to gain from each other. When we date someone or meet someone on a blind date, we assess the worth of the other person based on educational background and financial standing. We hope to marry someone with an attractive appearance, nice personality and high social status, in addition to their being totally in love with us. When young people say they fell in love at first sight, it means that the person they fell in love with seemed to possess all the qualities they were looking for in a boyfriend or a girlfriend. We never hear of people falling in love at first sight with someone who is poor,

physically disabled and a stutterer. The truth is, we usually experience love at first sight with people who look like princes and princesses in our eyes. However, interestingly enough, couples who were instantly attracted to each other usually don't stay together for a long time. The divorce rate for such pairs is higher than that of couples whose affection toward each other grew over time. What is the reason for this? When we fall in love at first sight, we tend to have high expectations of our loved one. However, since it is impossible for anyone to fulfill such high expectations, we inevitably become disappointed. When we have low or even no expectations of our partners, the relationship is more likely to last, and we are less likely to be let down. In other words, if our expectations are low, we will not end up hating someone with a vengeance, breaking up, or becoming enemies.

Bonding with someone and sharing affection with each other is not something that can be forced. Just because we love someone doesn't mean that person will necessarily reciprocate the emotion. Likewise, we cannot always like someone right away just because that person is interested in us. Sometimes, over an extended period of time, we become emotionally close to someone, or we grow to appreciate and like someone because of his trustworthiness. Especially when we are faced with a hardship, how our friends treat us can be an accurate measure of their genuineness and how much they value our friendship.

The phrase "Preserve your friendship with pure motives," doesn't mean we must be devoted to only one friend. It means that if we treat all our friends well with good intentions, our friendships will endure over time. We can become wealthy by being frugal and managing our finances well. However, we have to know that maintaining good relationships with people can also serve as a tremendous asset. Disliking someone or even becoming enemies with someone who was once a friend is equivalent to losing a valuable asset. The famous Korean Buddhist, Master Wonhyo[4] claimed that even when people dislike us, the source of the problem lies within us rather than in them. It is hard for us to reach that level of enlightenment. However, as Buddhist practitioners, we should at least refrain from hating others. Even if we have legitimate reasons to despise someone, such as suffering a financial loss because of him or being assaulted by him, we still should let go of the hatred toward him. When we hate someone, we feel bad and end up losing that person's friendship.

---

4. Master Wonhyo (617~686 AD) : One of the most eminent scholar-monks in Korean Buddhist tradition

Therefore, practicing diligently can be very lucrative because we, as practitioners, earn the friendship and trust of people around us, which in turn becomes our asset, yielding profits for us in one way or another. Any good deeds we do will eventually come back to us, as the seed of a good deed we sow will bear fruit someday. We may harvest the fruit right away or maybe 10 years later. Therefore, when we befriend someone, we should work on building a long-lasting relationship, and the only way to do that is not expecting benefits from the friendship.

The Buddhist teaching of cause and effect helps us realize there are no real gains or losses in life. If an investment we made does not yield returns right away, we feel as if we took a loss. On the other hand, if a small investment we made yields high returns, it feels as if we made a profit. In the short run, it feels as if we are continually either winning or losing ground. However, taking a loss for now is not necessarily bad because the longer it takes for us get the returns, the more "interest" they will have accrued, resulting in a bigger profit. Also, making a gain now is not necessarily good because we have to pay it back someday. Therefore, we should not dwell too much on either profit or loss. When we get compensated more than the effort we put in, it is equivalent to using up our savings or borrowing money, which we will need to pay back in the future. Similarly, when we get underpaid for the work we did, we can think of it as paying off a loan we had taken out in the past or putting more money into our savings. From an infinite time perspective, there are no gains or losses in life. If we keep this big picture in mind, we can lead a life of abundance without seeking to benefit from others.

Surround yourself with people who have different opinions from yours

Do not expect others to follow your wishes.

If they do, you will become arrogant.

Thus, the Buddha said,

"Surround yourself with people who have different opinions

from yours for your practice."

We all want others to follow our wishes. When we say something, we would like our spouses to agree with us, our children to listen to us, and our parents to fully support us. However, this is far from reality. In our everyday lives, it is normal that other people don't submit to our wishes since everybody has different opinions. As other people are entitled to their own outlooks, their views can differ from ours. Therefore, when we express our own opinions, we should do so lightheartedly. That is, we shouldn't expect others to instantly concur. Thinking it is a waste of time to talk to those who do not agree with us means that we want others to readily accept our views.

We might want others to agree with us unconditionally, but if they do, we will become very conceited. The best example of such arrogance is displayed by kings. From early childhood, a king is accustomed to having everyone around him obey his orders, so he mistakenly believes that everything he says and thinks is right all the time. Therefore, if someone disobeys him, the king gets angry and punishes the person. He may even take the life of that person right then and there. As an individual, a so-called "bad" king is actually an unfortunate human being. As a prince, he must have been groomed from an early age to give orders without ever having to listen to others. As a result, he ends up becoming a bad king despite his good intentions. When others acquiesce to your will, you become arrogant, and such self-importance will eventually make you unhappy.

Since more children these days are being raised in a similar way, as spoiled princes and princesses, it is safe to predict that the divorce rate will rise in the future. The number of people getting divorced more than once is also expected to increase. The influx of Western influence and the disappearance of the old traditional values are not the only reasons for the rising divorce rate in Korea. The most compelling reason for such a high divorce rate is, since the advent of the nuclear family in Korea, children are raised to be more self-centered than prior generations.

For example, parents often spoil their children by trying to give them everything they want even if they can barely afford it. A child who is raised that way may be described as having a strong personality but is actually ill-mannered and inconsiderate. When these children feel that their parents are not doing enough for them, they act rebelliously, protesting, "Why did you have me if you cannot do these things for me?" Unfortunately, the attitude of these children is the result of their parents' upbringing.

For example, parents who normally take the bus or an economy class train when they travel alone will employ a taxi cab or ride in a luxury train when they travel with their children because they want to give them the best. Since the children get accustomed to a cab or a luxury train from an early age, they feel resentment when their parents try to lower their standard of living due to financial hardship. These children are not the ones to blame; they were brought up in such a way by their parents. When I visited

Afghanistan and was invited to Afghani households, I saw children who looked to be only about five years old bowing to the guests, bringing drinks and helping their parents with various chores. They even shined my shoes and placed them in front of me when I was getting ready to leave. What about Korean children nowadays? It is the parents who usually get their kids' shoes and even help them put them on. Since these children are so accustomed to being pampered by their parents, when they go to school, where no one gives them the same care and attention, they feel that their school friends are selfish. I predict that in the future, genuine and long-lasting friendships will be rare since most children are being raised to be so self-centered.

Always having been at the receiving end and having been raised to be egocentric, today's young people have a hard time understanding the lives of their

parents or those of others, making the generation gap wider than ever before. This wide gap can be compared to the cultural difference between Christians and Muslims or that between Koreans and Japanese. On the other hand, aside from using different languages, Korean and Japanese youths share a lot in common and can bond easily with each other. Despite having the same language and physical appearance, the young and the older generations of Koreans share little else in common. Based on the current social changes in South Korea, it is safe to assume that there will be an enormous cultural disparity between North and South Koreans in the future. They won't have much in common aside from being the same race, speaking the same language, sharing similar physical features and the same traditional customs. This disparity will not result simply from the difference in their political ideologies. Rather, the vastly different pace at which the social changes are taking place in North Korea and South Korea will account for the discrepancies in their cultural values.

Given that others are different from us, we should express our opinions without assuming or expecting that they will agree with us. Likewise, if others have opinions different from ours, we should acknowledge them as their point of view, even though we do not necessarily agree. Furthermore, if we want to elaborate on our views, we can do so without insisting that others change their views accordingly. It is good to share our ideas, but if we insist that other people accept them, we are oppressing others. Everyone should express his or her opinions in a candid way, acknowledge the other's beliefs, and openly discuss it. If we agree, we can begin to collaborate. If not, we can accept the differences and decide to work independently. From this perspective, "Do not expect others to follow your wishes," is especially valuable among all the teachings in "Bowang Sammaeron." An enlightened person knows that it is foolish to assert his viewpoint. When we express our opinions, we should simply state them without evaluating in our heads whether they are right or wrong based on our values and views. Exchanging ideas easily with others means revealing our opinions as they are without suppressing them and also listening to the opinions of others with an open mind. It means listening to others without the pressure of having to accept their outlook. When talking, we should do it with ease, and do the same when listening. We should not have the mindset that others must agree with us or feel pressured to agree with them. Then, we will be able to listen to others more attentively. Any kind of judgment should come afterwards.

Finally, becoming arrogant will only make us unhappy. Just as it takes different types of trees to form a forest, if we can live peacefully with people whose opinions differ from ours, we have already made great advances in our practice. If we surround ourselves only with individuals who always agree with us, we form a clique. On the other hand, when we can live with people who disagree with us, it is an indication that we are quite advanced in our practice. I am not saying that we must avoid people who agree with us or that we should make an effort to spend time with people who disagree with us for the sake of our practice. However, when we do encounter those who oppose our views, we shouldn't make ourselves miserable by rejecting and hating them.

Discard the expectation of rewards

Do not expect merits for your good deeds.

If you do, you will work only for your self-interest.

Thus, the Buddha said,

"Discard the expectation of rewards

as you would throw away old shoes."

When we provide material goods to others, help those in need, or do something useful for society, deep inside our minds, we want to be rewarded. Although people often say that parental love is unconditional and selfless, parents nevertheless expect something in return from their children. When a child falls short of her expectations, a mother may lament, "After all the hardships I went through to raise you…" She is disappointed because her child did not fully meet her expectations, which is an indication that the desire for compensation exists even in the minds of parents who profess selfless love for their offspring. So, it goes without saying that people expect rewards for anything they do for non-family members.

"I did this for you," is another way of saying "you should recognize my efforts." In other words, any time I do something for you, you have to return the favor in one way or another, be it with verbal acknowledgement or with money. What happens when you have such expectations for rewards? Everything will be OK as long as the other person responds in the way you want. If not, you are bound to be disappointed. When there is an overwhelming disappointment, it takes on the form of hatred. Similarly, when hatred grows strong, a feeling of resentment sets in, and when the resentment continues, it becomes animosity. Once the animosity takes root in a person's heart, he will want to take revenge on the other person. Thus, what was once an affectionate feeling toward someone can transform to the point of wanting to hurt that individual.

When the Buddha was alive, there was a woman who came to admire him after listening to his Dharma teachings. She respected him so much that she made all kinds of offerings to him. However, when she realized that the Buddha treated her the same as everybody else, she became disappointed. This is because she wished that the Buddha would extend special treatment only to her. However, the Buddha always treated everyone the same. Eventually, her disappointment turned into hatred, so she stopped making offerings to the Buddha and no longer attended the temple. Sometime later, she married a prince, and in due time, she became a queen. One day, the Buddha came to her country to spread the Dharma teachings. When she saw that the court ladies were very happily listening to his Dharma talk, she was suddenly seized with jealousy. Unable to control her envy, she forbade the court ladies from listening to the Buddha's teachings and even persuaded the King to order a prohibition on giving food to the Buddha. This queen, who had once admired the Buddha, ultimately became his most powerful opponent in his efforts to spread the Dharma and went so far as to threaten his life.

When we like someone, it is our mind doing so. The person we admire is not actually making us feel the way we do. However, if that individual does not reciprocate our feelings, we end up resenting or even wanting to hurt him or her. Whereas unwise people revel in self-aggrandizement when others praise them, the prudent prevent future trouble by being careful not to get caught up in the euphoria produced by the admiration. When buds sprout in the Spring, wise people foresee that they will grow into big leaves in the Summer and eventually wither and fall in the Autumn. So, they are not sad when they see the leaves blow away in the Autumn wind. They already see the withered leaves in the new buds, but they enjoy the buds, the lush green leaves, and the withered Autumn leaves all the same. Once we realize that things are "empty" – have no fixed inherent qualities but change according to the condition – we can live in accordance with the principle of cause and effect. Since we can predict the outcome of our actions, we don't have to become attached to or ignore the result but simply accept it as reality. For example, when someone loves you and you love that person in return, there are inevitable consequences that will follow, so you should be prepared to accept them. If you are not, you should not let yourself be swept away by the feelings of the person who is infatuated with you. That is, you should accept that you are the object of someone's love, but you don't have to become attached to the other person's feelings and feel obligated to reciprocate.

We like the mountains, the oceans and the flowers but never feel any resentment toward them. This is because we do not expect them to do anything for us. Even when we climb Mt. Sorak or visit the ocean dozens of times, we still enjoy them the same. Since we don't have any expectations of them, we never harbor any negative feelings toward them. Some people worry that they may become stoic and lose zest for life if they practice Buddhism. This concern stems from a lack of clear understanding of Buddhism. Probing into the essence of the Truth, we realize that the source of the problem lies not in becoming fond of someone or something but in expecting something in return.

Inevitably, expectations will result in hatred. That's why the Buddha taught us to love without expecting to be loved back and to give without hoping to be repaid. If there is no expectation, there is no karma, and love would become neither the seed of tears nor the seed of hatred. In essence, hatred arises because we insist on things to be the way we want. According to the Diamond Sutra[5], "A bodhisattva gives without wanting anything in return." Thus, giving without expecting to be paid back is genuine merit. As a result, if you don't expect anything, no matter whom you like or what you give, you will never end up feeling indignation. Reflect on your feelings for the mountains,

5. Diamond Sutra : One of the most highly regarded and widely read sutras in Mahayana Buddhism. It belongs to the "Perfection of Wisdom" genre and emphasizes the practice of non-abiding and non-attachment.

the oceans or the flowers. Because you don't expect any emotional response from them, you never feel any resentment toward them, no matter how much you love them.

Then, why is it that we end up resenting someone we liked and willingly gave so much to? In human relationships, there are instances in which people give their money and heart to others but end up getting backstabbed by them and becoming enemies with them. They would have been better off if they hadn't given anything to them in the first place. Only when there are no expectations can there be no disappointments or hatred when you provide material goods, give help, or fall in love. Again, negative feelings emerge because we expect something in return from the person we have helped or loved. Think back carefully. How many people whom you have helped a great deal or loved deeply are you still on good terms with? There are many women in Korea who, after they got married, have helped their brothers-in-law or sisters-in-law with their school tuitions or provided room and board for them until they got married. Are they still on good terms with their brothers-in-law or sisters-in-law? Most likely, they are not, and perhaps they are not even on speaking terms now.

Again, this is because those women expected a great deal in return for all they did for their in-laws. Especially in the cases in which the wife has supported her husband through law school or an older sister has paid for her younger siblings' education, everyone involved inevitably ends up resenting one another. While the benefactors want to be compensated for their efforts, the beneficiaries do not show enough gratitude. As a result, the givers feel unappreciated and the recipients feel indebted and burdened. The recipients do not want to be repeatedly reminded of how much help they have received and be made to feel as if they owe everything to them. Understandably, they want to avoid meeting the people who helped them as much as possible, which in turn, makes the benefactors feel even more unappreciated. As a result, the two parties eventually end up despising each other. Ultimately, our expectations make us miserable and hurt our relationships with others. Adopting this principle, as Buddhist practitioners We should practice generosity without expecting anything in return.

Accumulate wealth through modest gains

Do not wish for excessive profits.

Undue profits inevitably lead to foolishness.

Therefore, the Buddha said,

"Accumulate wealth through modest gains."

When we venture on a business, we always hope to make a large profit. We want big rewards for small efforts. In the same way, we make meager offerings to the Buddha and pray, "Please help my son receive admission to Seoul National University, the most prestigious university in Korea." In addition, mothers often want daughters-in-law with outstanding qualifications even when their sons may have many shortcomings and equally good sons-in-law when their own daughters have numerous personal flaws. While it is understandable that parents want only the best for their children, they are being contradictory. If the mother knows that her son or daughter is a difficult person to live with, she should realize that it would be even harder for others to do so and should always be grateful to her daughter-in-law or son-in-law for putting up with her child. She should thank them, saying, "You are a good person for taking care of my son despite all his flaws," or, "I appreciate you providing for my daughter." This is the mindset that the mother should have. To her daughter-in-law, she should say, "If you had not married my son, he might have lived alone all his life. Thank you for marrying my son," and to her son-in-law, "Who would have married my daughter if it hadn't been for you? Thank you." When mothers-in-law show such an appreciation and provide assistance to their sons-in-law or daughters-in-law without meddling in their lives, there won't be any conflicts. However, they usually don't appreciate their children's spouses and thus end up disliking them and having conflicts. Praying without counting our blessings is like wishing for unreasonably high profits. Being unwise, we always want a lot more than we deserve.

We also behave this way with our business deals. When selling a product, we think of every conceivable way to get the highest price possible, and after we have sold it, we feel anxious that the value of the sold product might increase. On the other hand, when buying something, we want to pay the lowest possible price for it and worry that the price may fall after the purchase. This is how our minds operate. The Buddha never said people should not seek to make a profit. Whereas the Buddha told practitioners, "Never seek to benefit from others; only help others," he told lay people, "Do not hope to seek undue profits; if you are too greedy, you will invite trouble." This is the meaning of "Do not wish for excessive profits. Undue profits inevitably lead to foolishness."

Let's take a look at our society today. When people suddenly become extremely rich from stocks or real estate, instead of being careful with their money and using it for good causes, they tend to lead extravagant lives and waste their wealth on self-indulgences. We rarely hear of lottery winners who manage their money well and lead successful lives with their newfound fortune. In fact, it is hard to find lottery winners who are leading normal lives. This also applies to earning money from work. Being overly compensated is a source of trouble.

I once read in a magazine article that women who work in high-class hostess bars make about

$10,000 a month but spend all of it, so they have no money left to save. Even some college students who work part time at such places end up spending so much on beautifying themselves that they accrue debt rather than save money. Sadly, those college students experience mental and physical degradation. They are actually worse off than those who make $100 a month but spend only half and save the rest.

Once a person becomes a spendthrift, it is difficult to revert to being frugal. For example, if we normally ride the economy class train, buying an expensive business class ticket for the first time will make us feel uneasy. However, once we have tasted the comfort of business class trains, it is hard to go back to riding in economy. The same goes for riding taxis. If we get used to the convenience of taking a taxi, we won't ride the bus any more. When we plan to take the bus, we leave early enough so that we can arrive on time by bus for our appointment. However, once we get accustomed to taking a taxi, we idle away some time thinking that we can still make the appointment if we take a cab. Furthermore, once we get used to driving our own car, we can no longer go anywhere without it. Our cars become like our own legs. We can't even imagine going anywhere without a car because it would feel as if our legs were missing. All these behaviors are habits.

The nature of the habit is such that once we experience something more convenient or better than what we are used to, it is very difficult to revert to our prior lifestyle. If we happen to make a great amount of money from a business deal, after spending it, we again hope to obtain excessive profits. However, the probability of continually earning that kind of revenue is very slim. Consequently, we become distressed because we can't attain it easily. Even if we succeed in obtaining enormous profits, there are many side effects that accompany it. When things do not continue to go our way, we end up in greater distress than before.

Excessive greed leads to foolishness, which eventually leads us to the path toward self-destruction. As a result, we become physically exhausted and mentally impoverished. Although people indulge themselves in alcohol, cigarettes, and drugs for pleasure, they also become addicted to them in times of desperation. People with plenty of money can afford to engage in pleasurable pursuits for the sake of enjoyment.

When these people, however, are faced with extreme hardships, they are more prone to depend on such diversions in order to forget their pain. Therefore, it is said that neither Heaven nor Hell is a good place for spiritual practice.

Thus, the Buddha's teaching of "Do not wish for excessive profits, but become wealthy through modest gains," means that if we can be content with what we have, we can be the wealthiest people in the world. Rich people who are never satisfied no matter how much wealth they have accumulated should actually be considered poor, while poor people who are happy with what they have should be deemed rich.

If we are in constant agony over the things we lack and complain about things that do not go our way, we are leading a life of poverty. If we live frugally yet satisfied with our share in life, we are leading a life of noble poverty. Therefore, people who have chosen to live modestly belong to the wealthy class. Regardless of the amount of money they have, if they are truly satisfied with their lives, they are considered rich. Needless to say, it is important that we appreciate what we already have and refrain from expecting more than what we are due.

Regard unjust treatment as the door to entering spiritual practice

Refrain from defending your position

when feeling unjustly treated.

Defending your position will only make the other person

become resentful.

So the Buddha said,

"Regard unjust treatment as the door

to entering spiritual practice."

I used to believe rectifying injustice was an act of justice. However, there is a difference between clarifying falsehood and rectifying injustice. Whereas a lie can be objectively determined, one's sense of injustice is more likely to be subjective. We tend to think we are right most of the time, so all of us, at one time or another, feel we are unjustly treated. When people converse, it is impossible for their intended meanings to be perfectly conveyed. The reality is that the person we are talking to will misinterpret what we are saying to some degree. When the listener, after hearing the story, tells his version of it to others, we may want to defend our position and feel compelled to explain what we had intended to say: "I didn't say that. That is not what I meant." However, if we insist on correcting the misinterpreted version of the story, the listener, now in turn, feels accused of passing on an inaccurate account. Then, feeling wrongly accused, the listener wants to defend his position. This perpetuates a vicious cycle of accusations and justifications, increasing resentment between the two. Therefore, it is important to acknowledge that even though we say one thing, others can understand it to be another. If we defend our position by clarifying the misinterpretation, we may feel good, but the other person will feel bitter. This is how resentment can grow when one tries to clarify misunderstanding.

In a marriage, when the wife tries to point out and explain herself in every single situation in which she feels misunderstood or unjustly treated, the husband often feels hurt. Also, in a relationship between the mother-in-law and daughter-in-law, the former can get her feelings hurt if the latter tries to defend her position on every injustice she perceives. In these situations, the husband and the mother-in-law become the villains. They can try to explain and defend their positions, but that will make the wife and daughter-in-law feel wronged again.

Finding a way for both parties to co-exist happily is the purpose of practice. This is why the Buddha said we should regard the unjust treatment as gateway to practice. It is good to clarify serious misunderstandings, but we need to do so without making the people involved feel unjustly treated in the

process. If I kill a tiger because it killed my parents, my action would violate one of the Buddhist precepts of not taking life. However, if I kill the tiger in order to prevent it from taking more human lives, my action will be regarded as an act of a bodhisattva. The act of killing the tiger was done with the willingness to accept the consequence of taking life in order to save human lives.

When confronted with a difficult issue, if we readily accept the fact that we have a problem, the solution may become clear to us. Overcoming various obstacles and adversities in life can be viewed as practicing to become better at a particular endeavor we choose to pursue. If we can persevere and surmount difficulties that come our way, we will be able to accomplish anything we want. However, if we are sheltered like a plant in a greenhouse and only want an uneventful and safe life, we cannot learn anything. So, if unfortunate events keep happening in your life, think to yourself, "Something that was bound to happen is happening, and if I must overcome it sooner or later, it's better to get it over with now." If we need to pay off a debt, it's better to do so as soon as we can. There is no reason to defer the payment. If we face life with the positive attitude – "OK, if these are the consequences of my past actions, I am willing to take them right now."- we won't be afraid of anything that comes our way. Then, we will be able to fully understand the Buddha's teaching of "Achieve Nirvana amidst adversities."

Efforts to evade difficulties only lead to more problems. You will find the solution in the very obstacle you face. Thus, the Buddha found the path to Enlightenment amidst the obstacles. If people seeking the Truth cannot endure life's difficulties, they cannot surmount the hurdles in their practice and attain the treasures of the Dharma. Therefore, overcoming adversities leads us to the path toward Enlightenment.

We all wish to be healthy and financially secure. We want to be free of hindrance and temptation in practice, while we hope things will work out easily when accomplishing our goals. Also, we wish to benefit from our friends, have others always follow our wishes and make huge profits in our business transactions. Because we desire so many things, our lives are unhappy. We suffer because things don't turn out the way we expect. We yearn to be healthy, rich, and trouble-free in life. However, in reality, we get sick, experience financial hardships and encounter obstacles while trying to reach our goals.

Ironically, when we stop coveting so much, we can gain a different perspective and find the solution to our problem. Thus, amidst the obstacles, we can realize the Truth and experience a major turning point in our lives. In spite of such significant hindrances as six years of harsh asceticism and the rebellion of Devadatta, one of his disciples, against him, the Buddha was able to create and maintain a stable Sangha[6]. In the process of

---

6. Buddhist monastic order, traditionally composed of four groups : monks, nuns, laymen, and laywomen. The Sangha is a part – together with the Buddha and the Dharma – of the Threefold Refuge, the three treasures of Buddhism.

overcoming all kinds of obstacles, the Buddha found the path to Nirvana and showed us the way to a life of happiness and freedom.

Here is the story about when the Buddha and his 500 disciples were spending Vassa[7] in one of the kingdoms in India. The king of the land was so moved by the Buddha's Dharma teachings that he requested of him, "Please, spend the next vassa in my kingdom. I will provide food for you and your disciples for the entire three months." The Buddha agreed. The King, in the hopes of earning merits only for himself, forbade his people from offering food to the Buddha. Feeling content, the king fell into a sweet slumber. That night, he had a dream that his entire palace was covered with

7. Vassa is a three-month annual retreat observed by Theravada monks and nuns who, during this period, remain inside monasteries and temple grounds, devoting their time to intensive meditation and study. The tradition of Vassa began during the lifetime of Buddha because it was difficult for the Buddha and the monks to walk from village to village during India's long summer rainy season.

a white fabric. When he woke up in the morning, the ruler asked the Brahman to interpret his dream. Jealous of the king's devotion to the Buddha, the Brahman told him that the dream symbolized the possibility of losing either his life or his kingdom because of a rebellion unless he remained in isolation without seeing anyone for the next three months. Thus, the king declared that he would not meet anyone during that time period and prohibited outsiders from entering the palace.

The next day, the Buddha and his disciples came to the palace to obtain alms, but they were turned away. Since no one could meet the king, there was no way for those in the palace to verify the king's promise to provide food to the Buddha and his disciples. In addition, the people of the kingdom could not give any alms to the Buddha because of the royal order. Even though the ruler had not deliberately intended to deprive the Buddha and his disciples of food, they were left with no way to obtain alms. After a few days, a foreign merchant arrived at the kingdom with 500 horses in tow. When he heard about the plight of the Buddha and his disciples, the merchant felt compelled to do something to help. He said to himself, "Since I am a foreigner, I don't have to obey the king's orders. Although I don't have extra food, I have plenty of wheat bran for my horses. If the Buddha doesn't mind, I will gladly donate it." The Buddha and his disciples accepted the wheat bran and were able to complete their three months varsa. Even in this predicament, the Buddha neither blamed the king nor the people for withholding alms. For lay people, being at risk of starvation is an emergency situation; however, for the Buddha, it was neither a disaster nor something to avoid.

Obstacles are just a natural part of practice, work and even marriage. However, after overcoming difficulties, we may realize that they actually helped us advance in our practice. Many people sought the wisdom of the Dharma because their spouses or children caused them much trouble and pain. Once these people realized they had embarked on the path to the Truth thanks to their difficult family members, they began to regard them as bodhisattvas. They came to the temple thinking they were miserable because of others. However, now that they have solved their personal problems, they are grateful to those who impelled them to seek out the teachings of the Buddha. Thus, when we overcome an obstacle, it becomes a catalyst for our practice, but when we can't triumph, it becomes an insurmountable stumbling block, and we end up in frustration and despair.

Life is much like a hurdle race. If you jump over the hurdles, you win, but if you trip over them and fall, you lose. Thus, if you have an important goal in life, you should try your hardest to overcome the obstacles and achieve your purpose. There will always be complications in everything you do. Once you triumph over them, however, you realize they were nothing at all. For example, when you try to quit smoking, it is extremely hard, but once you quit, you wonder why it seemed so difficult in the first place. Thus, obstacles are only obstacles when you cannot overcome them. If you prevail over obstacles a few times, your confidence grows significantly, and you gain strength to cope with any problems.

Sujata Academy[8] in Dungeswhari in India is a

---

8. Sujata Academy : A school located in Dongheswari, India, which was founded in 1994 by Join Together Society (JTS), a relief organization headed by Ven. Pomnyun Sunim.

good example of achieving stability after overcoming various obstacles. The academy has been making steady progress for the past 15 years, but in that journey, there have been many incidents which almost forced the school to close permanently. About a year after the institution opened, a local thug robbed the school and scared all the teachers away, forcing the establishment to shut down. We were able to open the school again after several days of cleaning and repairs. The following year, we were faced with problems stemming from the students of different castes studying together, and the year after, there were internal conflicts among the teachers. Also, a few years ago, we even experienced the dreadful incident of a volunteer dispatched from Korea being murdered on the school grounds. In retrospect, however, these unfortunate events, rather than having adverse effects on the school, served as opportunities for improvement. Progress was made with each crisis we experienced. The local people, who were initially skeptical of our efforts, began to change their attitude and became supportive. They were moved by our dedication and perseverance in keeping the school in operation despite all of the adverse conditions. We don't know what other obstacles lie ahead, but we have come a long way from its inception to establishing Sujata Academy into the thriving school it is today.

If we keep in mind that obstacles actually help us mature and lead us to happiness, we can attain Enlightenment despite the difficulties we encounter in life. The Buddha arrived at peace by overcoming the obstacle. Also, the Ksitigarbha Bodhisattva[9] personally chose to place himself in "Hell" because he wanted

9. Ksitigarbha Bodhisattva : One of the most popular bodhisattvas in the Buddhist tradition, who brings relief and consolation to the suffering beings of hell.

to save all sentient beings there. This is the way of the bodhisattva, and this should be the attitude of all practitioners. If you have conflicts at home, instead of running away, try to resolve them as best as you can. When you have trouble with your children, please don't drive them out of your homes. Instead, listen to their problems with an open heart.

Any dilemma will be resolved when you try to see things from the other person's perspective and when you are wholeheartedly willing to do everything you can. If you avoid your problems, they become obstacles. However, if you actively make an effort to resolve them, they become the treasures from which you can draw your strengths. With this insight in mind, please continue to practice diligently.

One afternoon in the early winter of 1969, he had just finished bowing to the Buddha in the Dharma Hall and was in a hurry to get to his school as it was the final exams period. Then, the Abbot called him.

"What is it dear Abbot? I am busy today. I am on my way to school right now."

"Oh, you are busy today?"

"Yes. I have my final exams tomorrow."

"Where did you come from?"

"I was at school."

"Where were you before school?"

"I was at home."

"Where were you before you were at home?"

"........"

"WHERE WERE YOU BEFFORE YOU WERE AT HOME??"

"I was inside my mother's womb."

"Where were you before you were inside your mom's womb?"

"I don't know."

"Where are you going?"

"I am going home."

"Okay. Where will you go after you get home?"

"I have to go to school."

"Where will you go after school?"

"..........."

"WHERE WILL YOU GO AFTER SCHOOL?"

"I will die."

"After you die, where will you go?"

"I don't know. How would I know where I will be after I die?"

"YOU STUPID BOY! How come an IDIOT who doesn't even know where he came from and where he is going is so BUSY?"

"How come I am so busy when I don't even know where I came from and where I will go?" This koan led Ven. Pomnyun Sunim to begin his life at a Buddhist temple, and he eventually became a Buddhist monk. Since then, Ven. Pomnyun Sunim has completely immersed himself in the enlightening teachings of the Buddha. Based on these teachings, he offers guidance that has transformed the lives of countless people.

About the Author

Ven. Pomnyun Sunim* is the founder and guiding Zen master of Jungto Society. He is also an avid social activist, personally leading many projects supporting ecological awareness, human rights and world peace, and eradication of famine, disease and illiteracy.

Living up to the motto of Jungto Society, "Pure Mind, Good Friends, and Clean Land," Ven. Pomnyun Sunim has been advocating a new paradigm of civilization in which everyone becomes free and happy with daily spiritual practice, creates a congenial society through active participation in social movements, and protects the environment by adopting simple and earth-friendly lifestyles.

In his efforts to spread the new paradigm movement, he founded Join Together Society in 1994 to eradicate famine in developing countries; EcoBuddha in 1994 to protect the environment; and Good Friends in 1999 to support human rights, help refugees, and bolster world peace.

Also, he established The Peace Foundation, a private research institute, in 2004, to help bring permanent peace, stability, and unification to the Korean peninsula.

He has devoted much of his effort to advocating peace and ending famine, disease and illiteracy in many countries around the world including Afghanistan, India, Mongolia, Myanmar, Philippines, Sri Lanka, and North Korea.

In recognition of his dedication and achievements, Ven. Pomnyun Sunim was presented with the Ramon Magsaysay Award for Peace and International Understanding in September 2002.

Books and Commentaries - Korean

The Way to the Unification of the Korean Peninsula

The Harmony of Work and Buddhist Practice

Looking for Happiness in the World – In Search of a Hopeful Paradigm for Society

New Leadership for Future Generations

Buddhism and Peace

Buddhism and Environment

Commentaries I and II on the Diamond Sutra

Commentary on the Heart Sutra

The Frog Jumped Out of a Well

A Treatise for Young Buddhist Practitioners

Buddha – The Life and Philosophy

Engaged Buddhism

Eastern Philosophy and Environmental Issues

Prayer

The New Century

Enlightenment

Lecture on the Diamond Sutra

Books and Commentaries - *English*
True Happiness
True Freedom
True Wisdom

Books and Commentaries - *French*
Family

Books and Commentaries - *Japanese*
My Happy Way to Work

Books and Commentaries - Chinese

My Happy Way to Work

A Home Full of Laughter

Awards

1998 Kyobo Environmental Education Award, Korea

2000 Manhae Propagation Award, Korea

2002 Ramon Magsaysay Peace and International Understanding
      Award, Philippines

2006 DMZ(Demilitarized Zone)Peace Prize, Gangwon Province,
      Korea.

2007 National Reconciliation and Cooperation Award, Korean
      Council for Reconciliation and Cooperation, Korea

2011 POSCO Chungam Award, POSCO Chungam Foundation

2011 Reunification and Culture Award, Reunification and Culture
      Research Institute, Segye Daily

* Sunim : Buddhist monk is called "Sunim" in Korea

Jungto Society was founded with the aim of building a community of Buddhists who practice together and share the dedication to solve the problems that are prevalent in the modern world such as poverty, political and social conflicts, and environmental degradation.

While placing emphasis on personal transformation through individual Buddhist practice, Jungto Society has been supporting various social movements such as the advancement of ecological awareness; eradication of famine, disease and illiteracy; advocacy of peace and human rights; and the unification of the Korean peninsula.

Ven. Pomnyun Sunim and its members look into the 2,500 – year – old teachings of the Buddha to find the solutions for modern problems of this world. As Buddhists, its members view the environmental issues and the plight of people in the Third world countries with compassion and wisdom. They have been the active forerunners in various projects to help the people around the world including North Korea and many Third World countries. As of 2013, Jungto Society consists of 40 regional chapters in Korea and 19 overseas chapters including 11 in the United States.

About the Jungto USA Translation Team :

The Jungto USA Translation Team is a group of volunteers attending Jungto Society near their homes in various cities across the United States. Currently, there are seven active members volunteering their time and efforts to translate the Dharma talks of Ven. Pomnyun Sunim. Although the members vary in profession, gender and age, they share the common experience of having their lives transformed by the wisdom they found in Ven. Pomnyun Sunim's Dharma talks.

Having experienced the joy of turning their lives around to a positive direction, this team of volunteers has come together to translate the Dharma talks from Korean to English. They have devoted countless hours to translating this book, so that they can share the wisdom of the Buddha with English speaking readers. English translations of Ven. Pomnyun Sumin's books include True Happiness and True Freedom.